The Tagine Dream

Classical and Contemporary Tagines from Morocco, Tunisia, and Algeria

By
BookSumo Press

Published by
http://www.booksumo.com

LEGAL NOTES

Table of Contents

Preparing
a Tagine for Use

 Prep Time: 5 mins

Total Time: 3 hrs 5 mins

Servings per Recipe: 1
Calories   477.3
Cholesterol   0.0mg
Sodium   1.0mg
Carbohydrates   0.0g
Protein   0.0g

Ingredients
warm water
1/4 C. olive oil

Directions
1. Fill your sink or a kitchen basin with water and let your tagine sit in the water for 2 hrs.
2. Now rinse the tagine and coat the insides of it with olive oil liberally.
3. Place the tagine in the oven for 2 hrs at 350 degrees.
4. Enjoy.

RAS EL HANOUT
(Spice Mix)

🥣 Prep Time: 5 mins

🕐 Total Time: 5 mins

Servings per Recipe: 4
Calories	4 kcal
Carbohydrates	0.8 g
Cholesterol	0 mg
Fat	0.2 g
Fiber	0.3 g
Protein	0.1 g
Sodium	195 mg

Ingredients

1 tsp salt
1 tsp ground cumin
1 tsp ground ginger
1 tsp ground turmeric
3/4 tsp ground cinnamon
3/4 tsp freshly ground black pepper
1/2 tsp ground white pepper
1/2 tsp ground coriander seed
1/2 tsp ground cayenne pepper

1/2 tsp ground allspice
1/2 tsp ground nutmeg
1/4 tsp ground cloves

Directions

1. Combine salt, turmeric, cinnamon, black pepper, ginger, white pepper, coriander, cayenne pepper, cumin, allspice, nutmeg, and cloves in a small sized bowl thoroughly.

2. Store this in a container that is airtight up to 1 month.

Za'atar
(Spice Mix)

🥄 Prep Time: 5 mins
🕐 Total Time: 5 mins

Servings per Recipe: 1	
Calories	367.8
Fat	28.3g
Cholesterol	0.0mg
Sodium	18621.4mg
Carbohydrates	25.4g
Fiber	14.9g
Protein	1.7g

Ingredients

4 tablespoons ground sumac
2 tablespoons whole thyme
3 tablespoons toasted sesame seeds, coarsely ground
2 tablespoons oregano
2 tablespoons ground marjoram
1 teaspoon savory
1 teaspoon basil

2 tablespoons sea salt

Directions

1. Grab a mortar and pestle and add in: sumac, thyme, and sesame.
2. Grind the spices until everything is smooth then add in: the oregano, marjoram, savory, and basil.
3. Continue grinding everything until it is smooth.
4. Now add in the salt and grind everything again.
5. Enjoy.

HOMEMADE HARISSA
(Classical North African Style)

Prep Time: 20 mins
Total Time: 20 mins

Servings per Recipe: 40
Calories	28 kcal
Fat	2.8
Carbohydrates	0.9g
Protein	0.2 g
Cholesterol	0 m
Sodium	176 m

Ingredients

6 oz. bird's eye chilies, seeded and stems removed
12 cloves garlic, peeled
1 tbsp coriander, ground
1 tbsp ground cumin
1 tbsp salt
1 tbsp dried mint
1/2 C. chopped fresh cilantro
1/2 C. olive oil

Directions

1. Add the following to the bowl a food processor: chilies, cilantro, garlic, salt mint, coriander, and cumin.
2. Pulse the mix until it is smooth then add in some olive oil and pulse the mix a few more times.
3. Place the mix in jar and top everything with the rest of the oil.
4. Enjoy.

Homemade
Harissa (Classical Tunisian Style)

 Prep Time: 40 mins
 Total Time: 1 hr

Servings per Recipe: 192
Calories   10 kcal
Fat   0.3 g
Carbohydrates   1.9g
Protein   0.4 g
Cholesterol   0 m
Sodium   26 m

Ingredients
11 oz. dried red chile peppers, stems removed, seeds, removed
3/4 C. chopped garlic
2 C. caraway seed
1/2 tsp ground coriander seed
2 tsps salt

Directions
1. Let your chilies sit submerged in water for 30 mins then remove the liquids.
2. Now add the following to the bowl of a food processor: salt, pepper, coriander, garlic, and caraway.
3. Puree the mix then place everything into a Mason jar and top the mix with a bit of oil.
4. Place the lid on the jar tightly and put everything in the fridge.
5. Enjoy.

POTATOES
and Tomatoes Tagine

🥣 Prep Time: 20 mins

🕐 Total Time: 2 hr 10 mins

Servings per Recipe: 4

Calories	861.3
Cholesterol	56.6mg
Sodium	820.1mg
Carbohydrates	122.2g
Protein	47.8g

Ingredients

2 lbs monkfish
15 small new potatoes
4 tbsps olive oil
6 garlic cloves
15 cherry tomatoes
2 green bell peppers
1 C. kalamata olive
1/2 C. water
1 tsp kosher salt

2 tsps ground cumin
1 tsp paprika
1 lemon, juice of
1 bunch fresh cilantro, minced
1 loaf crusty bread

Directions

1. Remove the skin from your potatoes and cut them into chunks. Then take your monkfish and cut the fish into chunks as well.
2. Place your bell peppers under a preheated broiler and cook them until the skin chars then julienne the peppers once they have cooled.
3. Get a mortar and pestle and mash 2 pieces of garlic with some salt.
4. Combine in your diced cilantro, cumin, fresh squeeze lemon juice, and paprika.
5. Place some of this spice mix to the side and coat your fish with rest of it.
6. Place the fish in a bowl and place a covering of plastic on the bowl.
7. Put the fish in the fridge for 60 mins.
8. Get your potatoes boiling in water for 12 mins then slice them into two pieces.
9. Mince your garlic and begin to stir fry it in 3 tbsps of olive oil. Once the mix becomes slightly browned add the tomato and fry them until they become tender.

10. Now combine in the bell pepper, reserved spice mix, and some black pepper and salt as well.
11. Lay your potatoes into the bottom of a deep pan then top them with 3/4 of the garlic mix.
12. Now layer your pieces of fish.
13. Add the rest of your garlic mix and the olives as well.
14. Top everything with some olive oil then add in the water.
15. Get the mix boiling then place a lid on the pot and set the heat to low-medium.
16. Let the mix gently boil for 17 mins until the fish is fully done.
17. Top the tagine with some bread that has been toasted.
18. Enjoy.

CLASSICAL
Moroccan Honey Tagine

Prep Time: 45 mins

Total Time: 53 mins

Servings per Recipe: 6

Calories	1823.1
Cholesterol	224.7mg
Sodium	325.9mg
Carbohydrates	56.7g
Protein	24.1g

Ingredients

3 lbs organic beef, fat removed, cubed
1 tbsp olive oil
1 lb onion, quartered
4 garlic cloves, minced
1 lb carrot, peeled, chunked
9 oz. canned tomatoes
4 oz. dates, no pits
6 oz. prunes, no pits
2 tbsps honey

1/2 pint beef stock
1 cinnamon stick
6 tsps ras el hanout spice mix
salt & pepper
2 oz. toasted sliced almonds
2 tbsps fresh coriander, diced

Directions

1. Get your carrots boiling in water for 7 mins.

2. If you are using an electric tagine start to get it hot. If not set your slow cooker to high heat.

3. Sear your onions with olive oil and very high heat until charred.

4. Break the onion in pieces into the tagine or the slow cooker then add the carrots and garlic.

5. Add your beef cube to 2 C. of water and stir the cube until it is fully dissolved then stir in all the dried spice and the honey as well.

6. Stir the mix until it is smooth then pour everything into the pot with the onions along with the piece of cinnamon.

7. Add in your prunes, dates, and canned tomatoes. Then stir the mix to evenly distribute the ingredients.

8. Begin to sear your pieces of beef in hot olive oil until browned all over, in batches, then combine the meat with the ingredients in the pot.

9. Let the mix cook for 7 to 10 hours with high heat.

10. Eat this tagine with some couscous and top everything with the almonds and some cilantro. Enjoy.

Puff Pastry
Tagine from Tunisia

🥣 Prep Time: 1 hr
🕐 Total Time: 2 hr 15 mins

Servings per Recipe: 6
Calories   565.1
Cholesterol   320.5mg
Sodium   266.6mg
Carbohydrates   7.1g
Protein   43.1g

Ingredients

2 lbs chicken thigh
3 medium brown onions, skin removed & diced
1 tsp crushed saffron threads submerged in water
1 cup water
12 large rounds phyllo pastry
7 tbsps gruyere cheese, grated
4 large eggs, beaten

salt & ground black pepper
1 cup ricotta cheese, diced
egg wash (2 egg yolks stirred with 2 tsp veggie oil)
vegetable oil

Directions

1. Stir your onions in veggie oil for 4 mins until tender then add the water and the chicken.
2. Place a lid on the pan and let the meat cook for 50 mins with a medium level of heat.
3. Flip the chicken at least 3 times as it cooks.
4. Now set your oven to 375 degrees before doing anything else.
5. Once the chicken is done cooking remove the meat from the bone and throw away the bones and the skin also.
6. Place the chicken meat into a bowl and top the meat with: 3 tbsp of water, grated cheese, nutmeg paste, and saffron.
7. Stir the mix to evenly distribute the spices then add in some pepper, salt, and the whisked eggs.
8. Coat a pie dish with oil then place 5 pieces of pastry into the pan.
9. You want one third of the pastry to overlap the dish. Once you have added a piece of phyllo make sure you coat it with some veggie oil.

10. Place the sixth piece of phyllo in the middle of the dish.
11. Add some of the chicken to the pie dish then top the meat with some sliced ricotta then add the rest of the chicken.
12. Layer the overlapped phyllo over the chicken to form a pie.
13. Combine your eggs yolks and veggie oil to make an egg wash and coat the overlapped phyllo with the mix to seal it.
14. Top the dish with another piece of pastry and press the edges beneath the entire pie then top the phyllo with some of the egg wash.
15. Continue to lay four more pieces of phyllo and top each one with the egg wash as well.
16. Cook this in the oven for 15 mins.
17. Enjoy.

Bread
for Tagines

Prep Time: 1 hr 10 mins
Total Time: 1 hr 25 mins

Servings per Recipe: 1
Calories   581.2
Cholesterol   15.2mg
Sodium   878.4mg
Carbohydrates   102.0g
Protein   17.1g

Ingredients

2 1/2 C. semolina flour
1 C. unbleached all-purpose flour
1 1/2 tsps fast rising yeast
1 1/2 tsps salt
1 1/2 tsps granulated sugar
1 3/4 C. warm water
1 tbsp olive oil

2 tbsps unsalted butter, melted

Directions

1. Add the following to the bowl of a food processor: sugar, semolina, salt, regular flour, and yeast.
2. Pulse the mix a few times to evenly combine it then set the food processor to a low speed and add in your water in a stream then add the olive oil as well.
3. Combine the ingredients to form a smooth dough.
4. Knead the dough on a cutting board coated with flour for 10 mins then place a damp kitchen towel over the dough and let it sit for 20 mins.
5. Begin to knead the dough again for 5 mins then break it into 5 pieces.
6. Press down each piece of dough into a circle with a height of .25 inches.
7. Now set your oven to 400 degrees before doing anything else.
8. Cover a large baking sheet with parchment paper and coat the paper with some semolina then lay your flatten dough on it.

9. Continue doing this for all the dough.

10. Place a covering (damp kitchen towel) over the dough again and let everything rise for 50 mins.

11. Flatten the middle part of each piece of bread then use a fork to create some holes in it.

12. Coat each piece of dough with some melted butter and cook everything in the oven for 20 mins.

13. Cooking your bread on an oven stone will yield the best results.

14. Enjoy.

Classical
Moroccan Tagine II

🥄 Prep Time: 30 mins
🕐 Total Time: 2 hr

Servings per Recipe: 6
Calories   565.6
Cholesterol   108.8mg
Sodium   125.7mg
Carbohydrates   19.6g
Protein   27.7g

Ingredients

4 tbsps olive oil
2 lbs boneless lamb shoulder, cubed
2 medium onions, cut into 4 pieces
2 tsps ground cumin
1/2 tsp ground cinnamon
2 tsps sweet paprika
1 pinch saffron thread
salt & freshly ground black pepper

2 medium Yukon gold potatoes, cut into 4 pieces
1 large carrot, peeled, cut in 2 pieces, cut in 4 pieces
1 large zucchini, halved crosswise, cut in 4 pieces
2 small turnips, cut into 4 pieces
1 medium green pepper, julienned
1 medium tomatoes, diced

Directions

1. Sear your lamb all over in 2 tbsp of oil in a tagine. Once all the meat has been seared place everything to the side.
2. Add 2 more tbsps of oil to the tagine and being to fry your onions for 17 mins. Add in the saffron, cumin, paprika, cinnamon, some pepper, and some salt.
3. Stir the spices into the onions and fry everything for 4 more mins.
4. Now add the lamb to the onions and place all the meat and onions in the middle of the tagine.
5. Place your potatoes, zucchini, and carrots around the meat then place the green pepper and turnip in the same manner as well.
6. Top everything with some more pepper and salt then place the lid on the tagine.
7. Cook everything for about 90 mins and try to baste meat multiple times.
8. Finally place your tomatoes on top of the lamb and cook the tagine for 7 more mins.
9. Enjoy.

HONEY
and Beef Tagine

🥣 Prep Time: 20 mins

🕐 Total Time: 2 hr 20 mins

Servings per Recipe: 2
Calories   954.5
Cholesterol   99.0mg
Sodium   144.2mg
Carbohydrates   124.7g
Protein   29.6g

Ingredients

1 tbsp butter
1 tbsp olive oil
1 tsp ground cumin
1 tsp black pepper
1 tsp ground cinnamon
1/2 onion, minced
4 tbsps fresh coriander, diced
1/2 lb stewing beef, chunked
1/2 tsp saffron, soaked in

2 tbsps boiling water
1/2 lb stoned prunes
1 tbsp clear honey
1 tbsp sesame seeds, toasted
10 almonds, toasted

Directions

1. Melt your butter in a large pot then add in the onion, coriander and remaining spices.
2. Stir the mix and let everything cook for 1 mins.
3. Add the beef and stir the mix again.
4. Combine 1 C. of water with your saffron then pour this mix into the pot.
5. Get everything boiling, set the heat to low, add in half of the prunes, place the lid on the pot, and let everything simmer for 90 mins.
6. Remember to cook with very low heat to avoid burning.
7. Now add the rest of the prunes, the pepper, salt, and honey.
8. Let the tagine cook for 35 more mins then top everything with the almonds and sesame seeds.
9. Enjoy.

Kofta
Beef Kebab Tagine

Prep Time: 10 mins
Total Time: 35 mins

Servings per Recipe: 2
Calories   780.1
Cholesterol   136.0mg
Sodium   166.0mg
Carbohydrates   22.1g
Protein   42.5g

Ingredients

6 medium tomatoes, diced
1 tbsp paprika
1 tsp cumin
1/2 tsp cayenne pepper
3 tbsps parsley
2 garlic cloves, minced
salt and pepper, to taste

1/4 C. vegetable oil
1 lb ground beef
1 tbsp paprika
1 tsp cumin
1/2 tsp cayenne pepper
3 tbsps diced fresh flat-leaf parsley
2 garlic cloves, minced

Directions

1. Simmer the following in your tagine for 17 mins: tomatoes, paprika (1 tbsp), cumin (1 tsp), cayenne (.5 tsp), parsley (3 tsp), 2 pieces of garlic, some pepper, some salt, and 1/4 C. veggie oil.
2. Stir the mix a few times as it cooks.
3. Get a bowl, combine: ground beef, paprika (1 tbsp), cumin (1 tsp), cayenne (.5 tsp), parsley (4 tsp), 2 pieces garlic, some pepper, and some salt.
4. Work the spices into the meat with your hands then shape everything into meatballs.
5. Add the meatballs to the simmering sauce after 17 mins of cooking then set the heat to low and place the lid on the pot.
6. Let the meat cook for 12 mins then remove the lid and continue cooking everything for 5 more mins until the meat is fully done.
7. Serve the dish with some bread that has been toasted and top the bread liberally with the sauce.
8. Enjoy.

SPICY LENTIL
Chickpea, and Zucchini Tagine (Vegetarian)

Prep Time: 20 mins
Total Time: 1 hr 5 mins

Servings per Recipe: 4
Calories   414.9
Cholesterol   15.2mg
Sodium   299.7mg
Carbohydrates   68.9g
Protein   21.2g

Ingredients

2 tbsps butter
2 medium onions, diced
2 small fresh chili peppers, diced
1 tbsp paprika
1/2 tsp cayenne pepper
1 tsp ground cumin
1 C. dried lentils
4 tomatoes, diced
1/4 C. tomato puree

1 C. chickpeas, canned
1 C. carrot, diced
1 1/2 C. green beans, chunked
1 zucchini, diced
3/4 C. frozen green pea
1/2 C. flat leaf parsley, diced
1 tbsp za'atar spice mix
salt and pepper, to taste

Directions

1. Stir fry your chilies and onions in butter for 12 mins then combine in the cumin, cayenne, and paprika.
2. Stir the spices then fry everything for 2 more mins.
3. Now add in the tomato puree, tomatoes, and lentils. Pour in some water to cover the contents slightly and let the mix gently boil with a low level of heat for 22 mins.
4. Now stir in the green peas, chickpeas, zucchini, carrots, and green beans.
5. Continue to cook the mix for 17 more mins.
6. Place the mix in a large dish and cover the dish with some plastic.
7. Put everything in the fridge for 1 day then reheat everything and add the za'atar and parsley.
8. Enjoy.

Moroccan Lamb
and Saffron Tagine

🥣 Prep Time: 30 mins
🕐 Total Time: 2 hr 15 mins

Servings per Recipe: 4
Calories   599.8
Cholesterol   151.9mg
Sodium   323.2mg
Carbohydrates   16.2g
Protein   44.7g

Ingredients

2 tbsps olive oil
1 tsp ground turmeric
1 tsp ground ginger
2 lbs leg of lamb, chunked, fat removed
2 onions
1 C. chicken broth
8 threads saffron, toasted and crushed
15 fresh cilantro stems, bunched with kitchen twine

1 C. pitted prunes
2 tbsps honey
1 tsp ground cinnamon
1/2 tsp pepper
salt
1 tbsp sesame seeds, toasted

Directions

1. Get a skillet hot. Once it is hot add in your saffron threads and toast them for 4 mins.
2. Now place the threads into a mortar and pestle and grind them.
3. Add some salt and grind everything again.
4. Place the saffron to the side.
5. Begin to stir fry your lamb in olive oil then add in the ginger and turmeric.
6. Brown the meat for 4 mins then mince one onion and add it with the mix as well. Now combine in the cilantro, ground saffron, and broth.
7. Place a lid on the pot, set the heat to low, and let the contents cook for 90 mins. Then remove the cilantro.
8. Set your oven to 200 degrees before doing anything else.
9. Place all your meat into a casserole dish and place it in the oven.
10. Get the sauce simmering again then add the other onion after you have diced it.
11. Stir the onion in then add: the pepper, prunes, cinnamon, and honey.
12. Top the mix with some salt then let everything simmer for 10 mins.
13. Liberally top your meat with the sauce and garnish the entire dish with the sesame seeds.
14. Enjoy.

CLASSICAL
Pepper and Carrot Tagine

🍲 Prep Time: 20 mins

🕐 Total Time: 1 hr

Servings per Recipe: 4
Calories   302.9
Cholesterol   0.0mg
Sodium   518.9mg
Carbohydrates   61.7g
Protein   9.3g

Ingredients
2 tsps vegetable oil
2 C. onions, diced
2 large garlic cloves, crushed
1 C. carrot, sliced
1 large green bell pepper, julienned
1 tsp ground cumin
1/2 tsp ground allspice
1/2 tsp ground ginger
1/2 tsp turmeric

1/4 tsp cinnamon
1/4 tsp salt
1/4 tsp cayenne pepper
1 C. water
1 medium eggplant, peeled, cubed
1/2 C. raisins
1 (1 lb) can chickpeas, rinsed and drained

Directions
1. Stir fry your garlic and onions for 4 mins then combine in the spices, carrots, and bell peppers.
2. Add in half a C. of water and let the mix cook for 7 mins while stirring.
3. Now add the rest of the ingredients and place a lid on the pot.
4. Let everything continue to simmer for 32 mins.
5. Try to serve the dish with some cooked couscous.
6. Enjoy.

Classical Pepper and Carrot Tagine

Lemon, Dates and Red Lentil Tagine

🥣 Prep Time: 15 mins

🕐 Total Time: 55 mins

Servings per Recipe: 6
Calories	472.3
Cholesterol	0.0mg
Sodium	51.2mg
Carbohydrates	84.0g
Protein	23.5g

Ingredients

2 1/2 C. red lentils, well rinsed
6 C. unsalted vegetable stock
4 garlic cloves, diced
3 medium sweet potatoes, skin removed and cut into cubes
10 medium dates, seeded and diced
2 C. tomatoes, skin removed and diced
2 red bell peppers, peeled, cored, seeded, diced
2 C. onions, diced
3 tbsps fresh ginger, grated

2 tsps cayenne pepper
1 tbsp ground cumin
1 tbsp ground coriander
1 tbsp star anise
1 cinnamon stick
1 bay leaf
2 tbsps olive oil
3 tbsps fresh parsley, diced
salt and pepper
1 preserved lemon, rind of, diced

Directions

1. Stir fry the onions the spices in olive oil, in a large pot, until the onions are see-through.
2. Now stir in the lentils, ginger, and garlic.
3. Evenly distribute the spices then add the veggie stock and get everything boiling.
4. Once the mix is boiling set the heat to low and let the mix gently cook for 17 mins.
5. Now combine in the dates, sweet potatoes, pepper, and diced tomatoes.
6. Stir everything and continue to cook the contents for 27 more mins or until you find that the potatoes are tender.
7. As everything cooks add in more veggie stock if the Tagine becomes too thick for your liking.
8. Add some more pepper and salt and top everything with parsley.
9. Serve the tagine with the lemon for decoration.
10. Enjoy.

THE EASIEST
Tagine

Prep Time: 10 mins

Total Time: 40 mins

Servings per Recipe: 2
Calories	767.9
Cholesterol	139.2mg
Sodium	211.9mg
Carbohydrates	34.7g
Protein	49.5g

Ingredients
3 chicken breasts
2 cloves garlic, diced
1 small onion, sliced into rings
1 tsp turmeric
1/4 C. veggie oil
salt and pepper
3 carrots, cut into 4 pieces lengthwise
1 potato, cut into bite sized pieces
1 tomatoes, cut into wedges

olive, to garnish

Directions
1. Stir fry your garlic and onions with a low level of heat in your tagine, in oil.
2. Add some turmeric then add in the chicken and top them with some pepper and salt.
3. Place the lid on the tagine and brown all sides of the chicken. Then lay your carrots and potatoes around the chicken and pour in half a C. of water.
4. Place the lid back on the tagine and continue to cook everything with a low level of heat until the veggies are soft.
5. Now place your pieces of tomato on top of the meat and add some pepper, salt, and olives.
6. Enjoy.

Almonds
and Lamb Tagine

🥣 Prep Time: 10 mins
🕐 Total Time: 2 hr 10 mins

Servings per Recipe: 4
Calories   574.3
Cholesterol   133.8mg
Sodium   777.2mg
Carbohydrates   8.7g
Protein   41.1g

Ingredients

2 tsps paprika
2 tsps ground cumin
2 tsps ground coriander
1 tsp salt
1 tsp white pepper
1/2 tsp chili flakes
1/2 tsp ground cardamom

2 tbsps lemon juice
2 tbsps olive oil
2.5 lbs diced lamb
1 C. chicken stock
8 oz. pitted prunes
1/2 C. whole blanched almond

Directions

1. Set your oven to 350 degrees before doing anything else.
2. Get a bowl, combine: paprika, cumin, coriander, salt, white pepper, pepper flakes, cardamom, olive oil, and lemon juice.
3. Stir the mix to form a paste then cover your pieces of lamb with the mix.
4. Place the meat in the same bowl and place a covering of plastic over everything.
5. Put the meat in the fridge for 8 hrs.
6. Now brown the lamb all over in batches for 6 mins then add the lamb to a baking dish.
7. Add the stock to the baking dish once all the lamb has been browned.
8. Cover the dish with foil and cook everything in the oven for 60 mins.
9. Add in the almonds and the prunes and continue cooking the tagine for 60 more mins with no foil.
10. Eat the dish over cooked couscous.
11. Enjoy.

WINTER
Tagine

🥣 Prep Time: 5 mins

🕐 Total Time: 35 mins

Servings per Recipe: 2

Calories	426.6
Cholesterol	0.0mg
Sodium	940.4mg
Carbohydrates	59.9g
Protein	12.9g

Ingredients

2 tbsps olive oil
1/2 onion, diced
1 (15 oz.) cans chickpeas, drained & rinsed
1 (15 oz.) cans diced tomatoes
1 tbsp fresh Italian parsley, minced
1 tbsp fresh cilantro, minced
1/4 tsp salt
1/4 tsp black pepper
1/4 tsp harissa

1/4 tsp cinnamon
1/4 tsp turmeric
1/4 tsp ginger
1/4 tsp cumin

Directions

1. Stir fry your onions in oil for 7 mins then add in: cumin, ginger, turmeric, cinnamon, harissa, black pepper, salt, cilantro, and parsley.

2. Stir the spices into the onions and cook everything for 60 more secs.

3. Now add the diced tomatoes and chickpeas.

4. Stir the mix again then place a lid on the pot and cook everything for 35 mins with a low level of heat.

5. Enjoy.

Zucchini and Lemons Tagine (Vegetarian)

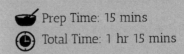

Prep Time: 15 mins
Total Time: 1 hr 15 mins

Servings per Recipe: 6
Calories   207.5
Cholesterol   0.0mg
Sodium   664.8mg
Carbohydrates   30.2g
Protein   6.2g

Ingredients

3 tbsps olive oil
1 onion, sliced
3 garlic cloves, diced
1 tsp ground coriander
1 tsp ground cumin
1 tsp paprika
1 tsp salt
1/2 tsp ground black pepper
1/4 tsp turmeric
2 C. vegetable broth

1 tbsp tomato paste
1 tbsp fresh parsley, minced
1 tbsp fresh cilantro, minced
1 (15 1/2 oz.) can chickpeas, no liquid
4 small carrots, peeled, sliced
1 green pepper, diced
2 zucchini, diced
3 tomatoes, diced
1 lemon, juiced
4 green onions, whites, minced

Directions

1. Stir fry your garlic and onions until everything is tender then combine in: the garlic, coriander, cumin, paprika, salt, black pepper, turmeric, cilantro, and parsley.
2. Stir the spices into the onions and cook everything for 60 more secs.
3. Now add in the broth and set the heat to low.
4. Stir in all the veggies excluding the garnish, any remaining herbs, and the tomato paste.
5. Stir everything evenly then place the lid on the pot and cook the mix for 50 mins.
6. Ensure that your veggies are soft, if not, continue cooking them for 10 more mins and add in half a C. of more broth.
7. Once the veggies are soft add your lemon juice and garnish everything with the onions.
8. Enjoy.

MEDITERRANEAN
Fish Tagine

🥘 Prep Time: 2 hr
🕐 Total Time: 2 hr 40 mins

Servings per Recipe: 4
Calories   486.0
Cholesterol   79.8mg
Sodium   542.1mg
Carbohydrates   17.3g
Protein   47.5g

Ingredients

1/4 C. flat leaf parsley, diced
2 tbsps fresh cilantro, diced
1/8 C. extra virgin olive oil
1 tsp ground ginger
2 tsps sweet Hungarian paprika
8 saffron threads, crushed
2 tsps fresh lemon juice
4 (6 oz.) red snapper fillets
4 large tomatoes, peeled, seeded, and diced
2 garlic cloves, minced

1 tsp ground cumin
1/2 tsp salt
1/4 tsp fresh ground pepper
1/4 C. extra virgin olive oil
2 large carrots, diagonally sliced
1 large onion, diced
1 tbsp preserved lemon
12 kalamata olives
fresh parsley, garnish

Directions

1. Get a bowl, combine: parsley, cilantro, olive oil, ginger, paprika, saffron, and lemon juice.
2. Lay your pieces of fish into a casserole dish and top them with the ginger mix.
3. Place a covering of plastic or a lid on the dish and put everything in the fridge for 4 hrs.
4. Flip the fish after 2 hrs.
5. Now get the following boiling in a large pot: cumin, tomato, and garlic.
6. Once the mix is boiling, set the heat to low, and let the mix cook for 10 mins then shut the heat and stir in the pepper and salt.
7. Begin to stir fry your onions and carrots in 1/4 C. of olive oil, in a Dutch oven for a few mins until the oil is hot. Then add in the tomato mix, place the lid on the pot, and cook everything with a medium level of heat for 14 mins.
8. Now lay your pieces of fish on top of everything along with the marinade.
9. Coat the mix with the lemon and the olives. Then place the lid back on the pot and cook the tagine for 12 mins.
10. Enjoy.

Florets
Tagine (Vegetarian)

🥣 Prep Time: 20 mins
🕐 Total Time: 48 mins

Servings per Recipe: 6
Calories   302.6
Cholesterol   0.0mg
Sodium   462.3mg
Carbohydrates   52.0g
Protein   10.9g

Ingredients

2 tbsps extra virgin olive oil
1 large sweet onion, diced
4 garlic cloves, diced
1 tsp ground cumin
1 tsp ground ginger
2 slices lemons
2 bay leaves
1/2 tsp kosher salt
1/2 tsp fresh ground pepper
14 1/2 oz. low vegetable broth

2 lbs cauliflower, cored, chunked
6 carrots, peeled, chunked
29 oz. fire-roasted whole tomatoes, undrained
15 oz. chickpeas, drained
1/2 C. raisins
1 cinnamon stick
2 medium zucchini, chunked
1/4 C. toasted slivered almonds
1/4 C. cilantro leaf
couscous, cooked

Directions

1. Stir fry your onions in oil, in a Dutch oven, for 8 mins then add in the pepper, garlic, salt, cumin, bay leaves, and lemon pieces.
2. Stir the mix and heat everything until aromatic.
3. Now add in the cinnamon stick, broth, raisins, cauliflower, chickpeas, tomatoes and liquid, and carrots.
4. Get everything boiling then crush the tomatoes.
5. Set the heat to low, place a lid on the pot, and let everything cook for 20 mins.
6. Try to stir a few times as it cooks.
7. Now combine in the zucchini and place the lid back on the pot.
8. Cook the zucchini for 12 more mins then layer the tagine and liquid liberally over the couscous.
9. Garnish the dish with cilantro and almonds.
10. Enjoy.

SUMMER
Time Tagine

Prep Time: 10 mins
Total Time: 40 mins

Servings per Recipe: 8
Calories   277.3
Cholesterol   0.0mg
Sodium   18.0mg
Carbohydrates   58.2g
Protein   5.6g

Ingredients

4 lbs potatoes, quartered
2 tbsps olive oil
2 onions, sliced
2 garlic cloves, crushed
1 tsp ground cumin
1 tsp ground coriander
1 tsp turmeric
1/2 tsp saffron strand
5 oz. large raisins

1/2 pint hot vegetable stock
2 tbsps diced flat leaf parsley
2 tbsps diced coriander

Directions

1. Boil your potatoes for 9 mins in water and salt. Then remove all the liquids.
2. Stir fry your onions for 5 mins in oil then add in the raisins, garlic, spices, and half of the veggie stock.
3. Get everything boiling, set the heat to low, and continue to cook the mix with a gentle boil for 7 mins.
4. Now add in the rest of the veggie stock and also the potatoes.
5. Continue cooking everything for 12 more mins. Then add in the herbs.
6. Enjoy.

Spiced
Onion Tagine

Prep Time: 10 mins
Total Time: 35 mins

Servings per Recipe: 4
Calories   266.3
Cholesterol   0.0mg
Sodium   5.9mg
Carbohydrates   21.3g
Protein   1.6g

Ingredients
1 1/2 lbs red onions, sliced
6 tbsps olive oil
1/2 tsp ground ginger
1 tsp fresh ground pepper
1 tsp cinnamon
1 tbsp sugar

Directions
1. Spread your onions in a casserole dish.
2. Get a bowl, combine: olive oil, ginger, pepper, cinnamon, and sugar.
3. Top the onions with this mix then stir everything in the casserole dish.
4. Place a covering of foil on the dish and let it sit for 3 hrs.
5. Set your oven to 325 degrees before doing anything else.
6. Once the oven is hot place the casserole dish into it and cook the tagine for 50 mins.
7. Now turn up the heat to 400 degrees and take off the foil.
8. Cook everything for 7 more mins.
9. Serve the mix over grilled or baked meat.
10. Enjoy.

OLIVES
and Lemons Tagine

🍲 Prep Time: 30 mins
🕐 Total Time: 1 hr 30 mins

Servings per Recipe: 4
Calories   221.0
Cholesterol   68.0mg
Sodium   1124.3mg
Carbohydrates   8.3g
Protein   17.7g

Ingredients

8 skinless chicken thighs
3/4 C. onion, minced
1/2 C. fresh cilantro, minced
1/2 C. Italian parsley, minced
2 garlic cloves, minced
1 tsp ground cumin
1 tsp ground ginger
1 tsp sweet paprika
1/2 tsp black pepper

1/4 tsp saffron, crushed
2 C. olives
1/2 preserved lemon, diced
1 lemon, juice of
salt
black pepper

Directions

1. Layer your pieces of chicken into the tagine and top them with: saffron, onion, half tsp pepper, cilantro, paprika, parsley, ginger, garlic, and cumin.
2. Now pour in two C. of water and place a lid on the tagine.
3. Set the heat to a medium level and get everything boiling.
4. Once the mix is boiling set the heat lower and gently cook the mix for 32 mins.
5. At the same time remove the pit from your olives by flattening them on a flat surface with a large spoon or knife.
6. Throw away the pits and combine the lemon juice, lemon, and olives in the tagine and let everything continue to simmer for 22 more mins.
7. Add some pepper and salt.
8. Enjoy.

Sweet Potatoes
and Sirloin Tagine

🥣 Prep Time: 15 mins
🕐 Total Time: 1 hr 45 mins

Servings per Recipe: 6
Calories	480.3
Cholesterol	111.0mg
Sodium	313.5mg
Carbohydrates	14.8g
Protein	34.3g

Ingredients

1 1/2 lbs top sirloin steaks, cubed
2 tbsps flour
2 tbsps vegetable oil, divided
1 (14 1/2 oz.) can chicken broth
1 medium onion, quartered
2 1/2 tsps ground cumin
2 tsps cinnamon

1/2 tsp ground ginger
1/8 tsp cayenne
1 bay leaf
8 C. sweet potatoes
1/2 C. raisins

Directions

1. Cover your pieces of beef with flour then fry half of the pieces of meat in a Dutch oven for 12 mins then place them to the side and fry the rest.
2. Now add all the meat to the pan and also add in all the spices, the onion, and the broth.
3. Get everything boiling then once it is, set the heat to low, place a lid on the pot, and gently cook the mix for 1.5 hrs.
4. Now add in the veggies and place the lid back on the pot.
5. Continue to cook everything for 20 more mins. Then add the raisins and stir.
6. Enjoy over couscous.

RUSTIC
Tagine

Prep Time: 10 mins
Total Time: 1 hr 40 mins

Servings per Recipe: 4
Calories   268.0
Cholesterol   68.9mg
Sodium   674.0mg
Carbohydrates   17.9g
Protein   23.8g

Ingredients

2 tbsps olive oil
1 red onion, grated
2 garlic cloves, crushed
1/2 tsp ras el hanout spice mix
1/2 tsp ground cinnamon
1/2 tsp ground ginger
1/2 tsp salt
1/4 tsp pepper
1 pinch saffron

1 tbsp lemon juice
1 (14 oz.) cans diced tomatoes
1 (8 oz.) cans tomato sauce
2 lbs skinless chicken leg quarters, separated
1 1/2-2 tbsps fragrant honey
1/3 C. water
1 tbsp blanched almond, to garnish
1/2 tbsp sesame seeds, to garnish

Directions

1. Stir fry your garlic and onions for 4 mins in olive oil, in a tagine, then add in all the spices and cook them for 1 more min until everything is aromatic.
2. Now add the lemon juice and tomatoes.
3. Top your chicken with pepper and salt then stir the meat into the mix.
4. Place the lid on the tagine and cook everything with a low level of heat for 65 mins.
5. Now add in half a C. of water and the honey.
6. Place the lid back on the tagine and continue to cook everything for 50 more mins until the meat is fully done.
7. Garnish the tagine with your sesame seeds and the almonds.
8. Enjoy.

Green Beans
and Lamb Tagine
(Algerian Style)

🥣 Prep Time: 20 mins
🕐 Total Time: 1 hr 40 mins

Servings per Recipe: 4
Calories   787.1
Cholesterol   163.3mg
Sodium   744.0mg
Carbohydrates   22.1g
Protein   42.3g

Ingredients

3 tbsps oil
2 lbs boneless lamb shoulder, chunked
1 medium onion, diced
4 garlic cloves, minced
1 tsp salt, to taste
1/4 tsp fresh ground black pepper
1 tsp ground cumin
1/2 tsp cayenne pepper

1/2 tsp saffron
4 C. water
1 1/2 lbs green beans, diced
2 tomatoes, diced
1 medium onion, sliced
4 tbsps parsley, diced
1 tsp ground cumin

Directions

1. Brown your lamb, garlic, and onions, in oil then combine in the turmeric, salt, saffron, pepper, cayenne, and 1 tsp of cumin.

2. Let the mix cook for 60 secs.

3. Now add your tomatoes and water and get everything boiling.

4. Once the mix is boiling, place a lid on the pot, set the heat to low, and let everything cook for 50 mins.

5. Stir in the beans and cook them for 12 mins then add in the onions, 1 tsp cumin and the parsley.

6. Let the mix cook for 12 more mins.

7. Enjoy.

TAGINE
for Autumn (Tomatoes and Pumpkin)

Prep Time: 15 mins

Total Time: 1 hr 5 mins

Servings per Recipe: 4
Calories	511.8
Cholesterol	0.0mg
Sodium	30.1mg
Carbohydrates	96.4g
Protein	25.8g

Ingredients
1 C. split peas
1 tbsp olive oil
1 medium brown onion, minced
3 garlic cloves, minced
2 tsps ground coriander
2 tsps ground cumin
2 tsps ground ginger
1 tsp sweet paprika
1 tsp ground allspice

2.5 lbs pumpkin, peeled, diced
1 can diced tomatoes
1 C. water
1 C. vegetable stock
2 tbsps clear honey
1/2 pound French beans, diced
1/4 C. roughly diced fresh coriander

Directions
1. Get your peas boiling in water with salt until they are soft then remove all the liquids.
2. Begin to stir fry your onion, in oil, until tender, then add the spices and the garlic.
3. Stir everything and let the garlic cook for 3 mins.
4. Now add the pumpkin and stir everything again to coat the pieces of pumpkin with spice.
5. Add in the stock, water, and canned tomatoes. Then get everything boiling.
6. Once the mix is boiling set the heat to low and let the contents gently cook for 22 mins.
7. Now add in the peas, beans, and honey then stir the mix.
8. Continue cook everything for 12 more mins until the beans are soft then shut the heat and add the coriander.
9. Enjoy.

Cabbage
Masala Tagine

🥣 Prep Time: 10 mins
🕐 Total Time: 30 mins

Servings per Recipe: 4
Calories   332.8
Cholesterol   0.0mg
Sodium   484.6mg
Carbohydrates   39.6g
Protein   6.8g

Ingredients

1/2 large cabbage, diced
1 lb green beans, trimmed
2 medium onions, diced
3 tbsps olive oil
5 garlic cloves, minced
1/2 tsp medium-hot hot pepper sauce
2 tsps garam masala
2 tsps dried basil

2 tsps sweet paprika
1/3 C. cider vinegar
1/3 C. broth
1 (28 oz.) cans crushed tomatoes, undrained

Directions

1. Stir fry your onion, beans, and cabbage in oil for 12 mins then add the garlic, hot sauce, masala, basil, and paprika.
2. Let the mix cook for 2 more mins then add in the broth and vinegar.
3. Get everything boiling and let the mix cook until no liquid remains.
4. Now add in 1 C. of water and the tomatoes.
5. Get everything boiling again, set the heat to low, place a lid on the pot, and let the mix cook for 12 mins.
6. Remove the lid and keep simmering the mix until everything becomes thick.
7. Stir the mix as you cook it uncovered.
8. Enjoy as an appetizer or over eggs.

TAGINE
for Breakfast

🥣 Prep Time: 15 mins
🕐 Total Time: 45 mins

Servings per Recipe: 6
Calories   133.8
Cholesterol   246.7mg
Sodium   93.4mg
Carbohydrates   10.9g
Protein   9.4g

Ingredients

olive oil
1 red onion, minced
1 tsp ground turmeric
1 tsp ground coriander
1 tsp ground paprika
10 tomatoes, skin removed & diced
7 eggs, beaten
1/2 C. coriander, diced
salt and pepper, to taste

Directions

1. Set your oven to 350 degrees before doing anything else.
2. Begin to stir fry your onions in olive oil, in a tagine, for 7 mins combine in the spices and continue to fry everything for 4 more mins.
3. Combine in the coriander and the tomatoes and gently boil the mix for 12 mins.
4. Shut the heat then pour in the whisked eggs and place a lid on the tagine.
5. Cook everything in the oven for 12 more mins.
6. Add some pepper and salt, then top everything with olive oil.
7. Enjoy.

Honey Harissa, and Eggplants Tagine

Honey

Prep Time: 10 mins
Total Time: 25 mins

Servings per Recipe: 4
Calories   187.3
Cholesterol   0.0mg
Sodium   12.0mg
Carbohydrates   30.5g
Protein   3.7g

Ingredients

2 tbsps olive oil
1 tsp cardamom seed
1 cinnamon stick
1 large onion, diced
1 large eggplant, diced
2 garlic cloves, crushed
2 tbsps harissa
1 can diced tomatoes

1/2 C. vegetable stock
2 tbsps honey, plus
extra honey, to drizzle
2 tbsps of fresh mint, diced

Directions

1. Fry your cinnamon and cardamom in oil for 1 mins then add in the eggplants and onions.
2. Continue to fry everything for 5 more mins then combine in the stock, garlic, tomatoes, and harissa.
3. Let everything simmer for 12 mins then add some pepper, salt, and the honey.
4. Stir in the honey and spices then shut the heat.
5. When serving the tagine top each serving with more honey and some mint.
6. Enjoy.

LAMB
Kebab Tagine

Prep Time: 20 mins
Total Time: 1 hr 20 mins

Servings per Recipe: 6
Calories   369.6
Cholesterol   218.9mg
Sodium   119.6mg
Carbohydrates   12.0g
Protein   20.2g

Ingredients

1 lb ground lamb
1 small onion, grated
2 tbsps diced parsley
1 tbsp diced cilantro
1/2 tsp cumin
2 pinches cayenne
salt, to taste
fresh ground black pepper, to taste
2 tbsps olive oil

2 medium onions, diced
2 lbs tomatoes, diced
2 garlic cloves, diced
1 bunch parsley, diced
1 tsp cumin
1/2 tsp cinnamon
1/4 tsp cayenne
1 tsp finely-ground black pepper
6 medium eggs

Directions

1. Get a bowl, mix: pepper, ground meat, salt, grated onion, cayenne, parsley, cumin, and cilantro.
2. Work the mix with your hands then shape everything into balls.
3. Brown your meatballs all over, in hot oil olive oil, in your tagine, then place them to the side.
4. Now add in the pepper, diced onions, cayenne, tomatoes, cinnamon, cumin, garlic, and parsley.
5. Let the mix cook for 32 mins then stir in the meatballs and get everything gently boiling.
6. Let the meat balls cook for 12 mins then break your eggs directly into the tagine to cook them for 6 mins.
7. Enjoy.

Fathia's Favorite
Tagine

Prep Time: 30 mins
Total Time: 1 hr 15 mins

Servings per Recipe: 8
Calories   214.9
Cholesterol   159.4mg
Sodium   296.5mg
Carbohydrates   21.8g
Protein   9.2g

Ingredients

1/4 C. extra virgin olive oil
1 medium onion, diced
1 bunch parsley, diced (about 11/4 C. packed)
6 canned artichoke hearts, drained cut in 4 pieces
1 1/2 C. mashed potatoes
1 C. soft white breadcrumb
6 large eggs, beaten
1 tsp bottled minced garlic

1 tsp cayenne pepper
salt

Directions

1. Coat a baking dish with nonstick spray.
2. Then begin to stir fry your parsley and onion, until the onions are see-through then add in the artichokes and get everything hot.
3. Get a bowl, mix: garlic, potatoes, eggs, and breadcrumbs.
4. Add in some salt, cayenne, and the onion mix.
5. Place everything into the baking dish evenly and cook the tagine in the oven for 40 mins.
6. Enjoy.

OLIVES, VEAL
and Lemon Tagine

🥣 Prep Time: 10 mins

🕐 Total Time: 1 hr 10 mins

Servings per Recipe: 4

Calories	216.9
Cholesterol	70.4mg
Sodium	479.0mg
Carbohydrates	12.1g
Protein	17.9g

Ingredients

12 oz. veal
12 purple olives
1 onion, minced
1/2 tsp salt
1/4 tsp pepper
1 tsp ginger, ground
1 tomatoes, diced
2 tsps coriander, diced
1 small sweet potato, slice in 4 lengthwise

1 tbsp olive oil
2 slices crystallized lemons, cut in half
1 tbsp lemon juice

Directions

1. Get a bowl, combine: lemon juice, crystal lemons, olive oil, coriander, tomatoes, ginger, pepper, salt, diced onions, and veal.

2. Let mix sit covered in the fridge for 60 mins then place everything into your tagine evenly.

3. Now set your oven to 360 degrees before doing anything else.

4. Place the lid on the tagine and cook everything in the oven for 60 more mins.

5. Now combine in the olives and continue baking the tagine for 12 mins with the lid removed.

6. Enjoy.

Fathia's Favorite
Tagine

Prep Time: 30 mins
Total Time: 1 hr 15 mins

Servings per Recipe: 8
Calories   214.9
Cholesterol   159.4mg
Sodium   296.5mg
Carbohydrates   21.8g
Protein   9.2g

Ingredients

1/4 C. extra virgin olive oil
1 medium onion, diced
1 bunch parsley, diced (about 1 1/4 C. packed)
6 canned artichoke hearts, drained cut in 4 pieces
1 1/2 C. mashed potatoes
1 C. soft white breadcrumb
6 large eggs, beaten
1 tsp bottled minced garlic

1 tsp cayenne pepper
salt

Directions

1. Coat a baking dish with nonstick spray.
2. Then begin to stir fry your parsley and onion, until the onions are see-through then add in the artichokes and get everything hot.
3. Get a bowl, mix: garlic, potatoes, eggs, and breadcrumbs.
4. Add in some salt, cayenne, and the onion mix.
5. Place everything into the baking dish evenly and cook the tagine in the oven for 40 mins.
6. Enjoy.

GINGER
and Fish Tagine

Prep Time: 15 mins
Total Time: 45 mins

Servings per Recipe: 8
Calories   479.4
Cholesterol   55.6mg
Sodium   879.3mg
Carbohydrates   37.5g
Protein   42.9g

Ingredients
1 lemon, halved
1/2 C. olive oil
1 lb onion, diced
8 large garlic cloves, diced
3 tbsps grated lemon peel
2 tsps paprika
1 1/2 tsps ground cumin
1 1/2 tsps ground ginger
1/4 tsp cayenne pepper

8 tbsps fresh parsley, diced
dill, to taste
8 tbsps of fresh mint, diced
3 lbs halibut
4 C. vegetable broth or 4 C. chicken broth
6 medium artichoke hearts
3 fresh fennel bulbs, trimmed, quartered vertically
5 large carrots, peeled, cut into 1 inch lengths

Directions
1. Stir fry your onions for 7 mins in 1/4 a C. of oil then add in the garlic, lemon peel, paprika, cumin, ginger, and cayenne.
2. Also add 6 tbsp of the following: mint, dill, and parsley.
3. Stir the spices and fry everything for 4 more mins.
4. Combine in the carrots, broth, artichokes, and fennel.
5. Get everything boiling, place a lid on the pot, set the heat to low, and let the mix gently cook for 17 mins.
6. Now remove the lid and continue to cook everything for 17 more mins.
7. Add in some pepper and salt and stir the mix.
8. Now set your oven to 400 degrees before doing anything else.
9. Once the oven is hot add the fish to casserole dish coated with nonstick spray then top the fish with the tagine.
10. Place a covering of foil on the dish and cook everything in the oven for 35 mins.
11. Enjoy.

Chicken
Tagine

Prep Time: 15 mins

Total Time: 1 hr 25 mins

Servings per Recipe: 6

Calories	717.1
Cholesterol	103.5mg
Sodium	1778.1mg
Carbohydrates	16.4g
Protein	27.3g

Ingredients

3 lbs chicken thighs
4 large onions, minced
4 garlic cloves, minced
1 tbsp fresh ginger, grated
1/2 C. olive oil
1 tbsp fresh parsley, diced
1 tbsp cilantro, diced
1 tbsp harissa
1/2 tsp cinnamon

1 tsp turmeric
1/2 tsp paprika
1/2 C. lemon juice
2 C. water
1 tbsp salt
1 tbsp black pepper
1 preserved lemon
1 (8 oz.) cans olives, minced

Directions

1. Add the following to your tagine: lemon juice, onions, paprika, garlic, turmeric, ginger, cinnamon, olive oil, harissa, cilantro, and parsley.
2. Stir the spices then add in your chicken and stir everything again to evenly coat the meat.
3. Place the lid on the tagine and put everything in the fridge for 8 hrs.
4. Add the water to the pot and the pepper and salt. Then get the mix boiling on the stove, set the heat to low, and let everything gently cook for 37 mins until the chicken is fully done.
5. At the same time get your lemon and olives boiling for 12 mins then remove any remaining liquids.
6. Combine the olives with the tagine and cook everything for 6 more mins.
7. Enjoy.

SWEET POTATOES
and Mint Tagine

Prep Time: 10 mins
Total Time: 1 hr 10 mins

Servings per Recipe: 4
Calories	642.8
Cholesterol	7.6mg
Sodium	190.2mg
Carbohydrates	129.7g
Protein	8.8g

Ingredients

3 tbsps olive oil
1 tbsp butter
25 white pearl onions, blanched and skin removed
2 lb sweet potatoes, skin removed and chunked
3 carrots, skin removed and chunked
1/3 lb ready to eat prunes
1 tsp ground cinnamon
1/2 tsp ground ginger
2 tsps clear honey
2 C. vegetable stock
1/4 C. diced fresh coriander
1/4 C. diced of fresh mint

Directions

1. Set your oven to 400 degrees before doing anything else.
2. Stir fry your onions for 7 mins in butter and olive oil then place half to the side.
3. Combine in the carrots and potatoes and brown them. Then add in the honey, prunes, ginger, and cinnamon.
4. Stir the mix then add the stock.
5. Place everything into a baking dish and cook the tagine in the oven for 50 mins.
6. Then add the rest of the onions and continue baking the tagine for 12 more mins. Add in the herbs and stir everything again.
7. Enjoy.

Mediterranean
Tagine

Prep Time: 15 mins
Total Time: 1 hr 25 mins

Servings per Recipe: 2
Calories   380.7
Cholesterol   0.0mg
Sodium   947.9mg
Carbohydrates   67.1g
Protein   14.2g

Ingredients

1 tsp canola oil
1 tsp olive oil
1/2-3/4 large onion, diced
1/4 yellow bell pepper, diced
1/4 red bell pepper, diced
1/4 orange bell pepper, diced
1/2 big tomatoes, cut into 4 pieces
2 garlic cloves, skin removed
1/4 C. fresh parsley
1/4 C. fresh cilantro
1 (15 oz.) cans diced tomatoes

1 (15 oz.) cans chickpeas, drained and rinsed
1/2 tsp turmeric
1/2 tsp ground coriander
1/2 tsp ground pepper
1/4-1/2 tsp salt
1/4 tsp ground ginger
1/4 tsp ground paprika
1/8-1/4 tsp cinnamon
1/8-1/4 tsp cayenne
3 pieces salmon

Directions

1. Stir fry your peppers and onions in canola and olive oil, in a tagine, until tender.
2. At the same time puree the following with a food processor: tomato, cilantro, garlic, and parsley.
3. Add this mix to the onions and also add in the canned tomatoes.
4. Stir the mix then add the chickpeas and the spices.
5. Stir the mix again then layer your pieces of fish over everything.
6. Push the fish into the mix then place a lid on the tagine.
7. Cook everything for 60 mins with a medium level of heat.
8. Enjoy.

APRICOTS, HONEY
and Squash Tagine

🥣 Prep Time: 45 mins

🕐 Total Time: 2 hr 45 mins

Servings per Recipe: 4
Calories   540.3
Cholesterol   120.0mg
Sodium   572.7mg
Carbohydrates   43.2g
Protein   34.8g

Ingredients

2 lbs cubed lamb
1 tbsp vegetable oil
1 large onion, diced
1 1/2 C. water
1 pinch saffron thread, crumbled
3/4 tsp salt
1/4 tsp black pepper
1 1/2 large carrots, cut into 1/4-inch-thick rounds
1 small sweet potato, skin removed and cut into 3/4-inch

pieces
3/4 tsp ground ginger
1/8 tsp cinnamon
2/3 C. pitted prune
1/2 C. dried apricot
1 medium yellow squash, cut into 3/4-inch pieces
2 tsps honey
freshly grated nutmeg

Directions

1. Sear half of your meat in 1/2 tsp of oil then place it to the side then sear the rest of the meat.
2. Add half a tsp more of oil to the tagine and begin to stir fry your onions until they are tender then add the meat back in.
3. Also add in the pepper, salt, saffron, and water.
4. Get everything boiling, set the heat to low, and place a lid on the tagine.
5. Let the mix cook for 90 mins then place the lamb on a serving dish.
6. Add the sweet potatoes and carrots to the tagine and cook the veggies, with the lid on the pot, for 12 mins then stir in the squash, ginger, apricots, cinnamon, and prunes.
7. Continue cooking the new veggies for 7 mins then add the meat back in also the honey.
8. Stir the honey into the tagine then add the nutmeg, more pepper, and more salt.
9. Let the tagine cook for 7 more mins with no lid.
10. Enjoy.

Brown
Rice Tagine

Prep Time: 0 mins
Total Time: 40 mins

Servings per Recipe: 6
Calories   426.0
Cholesterol   46.8mg
Sodium   316.2mg
Carbohydrates   55.7g
Protein   24.7g

Ingredients

2 tsps vegetable oil
1 onion, diced
3 garlic cloves, minced
1 lb extra lean ground beef
3/4 tsp allspice
3/4 tsp cinnamon
1 C. brown rice
2 C. chicken broth

1 sweet red pepper, diced
1 yellow pepper, diced
1 C. dried apricots
3 tbsps minced of fresh mint
2 tbsps fresh lemon juice
1/2 C. raw sunflower seeds

Directions

1. Begin to stir fry your garlic and onions in a Dutch oven for 2 mins then add in the beef and cook the meat for 7 mins while breaking it into pieces with a large spoon.
2. Now add the broth, rice, allspice and cinnamon.
3. Stir the spices into the broth and get everything boiling.
4. Place a lid on the pot and let the mix gently boil, with a medium level of heat, for 42 mins.
5. Once the rice is done add in the lemon juice, sweet peppers, mint, and dried fruit.
6. Shut the heat and garnish each serving with sunflower.
7. Enjoy.

TAGINE
Layered and Baked

🥄 Prep Time: 30 mins
🕐 Total Time: 1 hr 30 mins

Servings per Recipe: 6
Calories   279.5
Cholesterol   114.7mg
Sodium   549.3mg
Carbohydrates   19.7g
Protein   28.7g

Ingredients

2 tbsps olive oil
1 small eggplant, skin removed and cut into 1/2-inch dice (1/2 lb.)
1 medium zucchini, cut into 1/2-inch dice
1 onion, diced
3 garlic cloves, minced
1 1/2 lbs ground chicken
1 C. cooked couscous
1 C. firm white breadcrumb
1/2 C. diced flat leaf parsley

1/2 C. diced cilantro
1 tbsp grated fresh ginger
2 tsps grated lemon peel
2 tsps grated orange peel
1 tsp ground cumin
1 tsp salt
1/2 tsp fresh ground pepper
1/4 tsp cayenne
1/4 tsp ground cinnamon
1 egg

Directions

1. Set your oven to 350 degrees before doing anything else.
2. Begin to fry your garlic eggplants, onions, and zucchini for 13 mins in hot oil.
3. Get a bowl, combine: cooked veggies, chicken, egg, couscous, cinnamon, bread crumbs, cayenne, parsley, pepper, cilantro, salt, ginger, cumin, lemon pepper, and orange peels.
4. Lay the mix into a bread pan evenly and cook everything in the oven for 65 mins.
5. Enjoy.

Cinnamon
Chickpea Tagine

🥄 Prep Time: 30 mins
🕐 Total Time: 1 hr 10 mins

Servings per Recipe: 4
Calories   352.0
Cholesterol   0.0mg
Sodium   191.4mg
Carbohydrates   60.5g
Protein   10.0g

Ingredients
2 tbsps extra virgin olive oil
1 onion, diced
2 garlic cloves, minced
one 1-inch piece ginger, skin removed and minced
1 1/2 tsps ground cumin
2 tsps ground turmeric
6 cinnamon sticks
1/3 C. diced dried apricots
1 1/2 C. tomatoes, diced

2 C. vegetable stock
1 C. drained chickpeas
2 medium carrots, cut into bite-size chunks (optional)
2 zucchini, cut into bite-size chunks (optional)
salt and pepper
1 C. pearl couscous

Directions
1. For 5 mins stir fry your onions, in oil, in a pot, with a cover.
2. Now add in the cinnamon sticks, garlic, turmeric, ginger, and cumin.
3. Stir fry the spices for 3 mins then combine in: some salt, the dried fruit, zucchini, tomato, carrots, stock, some pepper, and the chickpeas.
4. Get the mix boiling, set the heat to low, and continue cooking everything with a gentle boil until the veggies are soft.
5. Once the veggies are soft pour in the couscous and cook it for 12 mins.
6. Enjoy.

TAGINE
for Canada

Prep Time: 30 mins
Total Time: 2 hr

Servings per Recipe: 2
Calories   926.6
Cholesterol   0.0mg
Sodium   298.3mg
Carbohydrates   78.1g
Protein   23.4g

Ingredients
4 duck legs, fat trimmed (or chicken legs)
2 tbsps olive oil
3 brown onions, diced
1/2 tsp ground turmeric
1 tsp sugar
1/2 tsp white pepper
1 tsp ground coriander
1/2 tsp ground ginger
salt and pepper
5 oz. almonds, blanched and roasted

1 oz. toasted sesame seeds
4 granny smith apples, peeled, core removed, sliced
2 tsp orange blossom water or 2 tsp water

Directions
1. Top your pieces of duck with pepper and salt. Brown the duck all over in oil for 7 mins then combine in the ginger and coriander.
2. Add in enough water to cover the meat and get everything boiling.
3. Once the mix is boiling, place a lid on the pot, set the heat to low, and let everything cook for 50 mins.
4. Now remove the duck and place it to the side. Also remove any fat in the pot.
5. Layer your onions in a tagine pot then place the duck on top in the middle. Pour 1/4 of the stock to the tagine pot place a lid on the pot and cook everything for 12 mins with a low level of heat.
6. Now add your apples around the duck.
7. Place a lid on the tagine pot and cook everything for 7 more mins.
8. Stir in your almonds, and blossom water. Garnish each serving with the sesame seeds.
9. Enjoy.

Classical
Arabic Tagine

🥣 Prep Time: 35 mins

🕐 Total Time: 1 hr

Servings per Recipe: 4

Calories	276.6
Cholesterol	66.3mg
Sodium	466.5mg
Carbohydrates	17.0g
Protein	36.0g

Ingredients

1 1/2 lbs halibut, rinsed and cleaned
1 onion, sliced thin
1 carrot, sliced thin
1 C. fresh cilantro, diced
10 garlic cloves, minced
2 tbsps gingerroot, fresh, grated
4 tsps ground cumin
1 C. lemon juice, fresh squeezed

1 chile, minced, seeds removed
2 tomatoes, diced
1/2 tsp salt

Directions

1. Set your oven to 350 degrees before doing anything else.
2. Coat a casserole dish with nonstick spray than layer your onions and carrots in the dish.
3. Place the pieces of fish on top and coat everything with some salt.
4. Add the following to the bowl of a food processor and puree it: half of the diced tomatoes, cilantro, chili, garlic, lemon juice, some salt, ginger, and cumin.
5. Top your fish with the puree and the rest of the tomatoes.
6. Place a covering of foil around the dish and cook everything in the oven for 20 mins.
7. Enjoy.

OCTOBER
Tagine

🥣 Prep Time: 10 mins

🕐 Total Time: 40 mins

Servings per Recipe: 4

Calories	300.9
Cholesterol	81.7mg
Sodium	1287.9mg
Carbohydrates	36.9g
Protein	22.4g

Ingredients
1 lb turkey ham, cubed
1 tsp curry powder
1/2 tsp cinnamon
1/2 tsp ground ginger
1/2 tsp olive oil
1 clove garlic, diced
2 C. nonfat beef broth
1 large sweet potato, chunked
1 large white onion, chunked
15 halved pitted prunes

1 inch lemon, zest
1 1/2 C. water
1/2 tsp ground coriander
1/8 tsp ground turmeric
2 tbsps slivered almonds
2 tbsps diced fresh cilantro

Directions
1. Get a bowl, combine: ginger, turkey, cinnamon, and curry.
2. Begin to stir fry your garlic, in oil, in a Dutch oven, for 3 mins, then combine in the turkey mix and the broth.
3. Get everything boiling.
4. Once the mix is boiling add in the lemon zest, sweet potatoes, prunes, and onions.
5. Place a lid on the pot, set the heat to low, and let the mix cook for 30 min.
6. Stir everything and continue cooking it for 5 more mins with no cover.
7. Now get your couscous boiling in water then shut the heat and add in the almonds, turmeric, and coriander.
8. Place a lid on the couscous and let everything sit for 10 mins. Then stir in the cilantro.
9. Serve your couscous under the tagine.
10. Enjoy.

Umm's
Favorite Tagine

Prep Time: 15 mins
Total Time: 40 mins

Servings per Recipe: 4
Calories   643.9
Cholesterol   299.4mg
Sodium   556.8mg
Carbohydrates   16.6g
Protein   28.4g

Ingredients

1 lb ground lamb
1 1/2 tbsps ground cumin
1 1/2 tbsps paprika
salt and pepper, to taste
4 tbsps butter
2 tbsps olive oil
4 garlic cloves, minced
1 large yellow onion, minced
1 tsp crushed red pepper flakes

1/2 tsp ground ginger
1/2 tsp saffron, crushed
1 bay leaf
1 (28 oz.) can tomatoes with juice, drained
4 eggs
1/2 C. kalamata olives, pits removed
1/4 C. parsley, minced

Directions

1. Get a bowl, combine: pepper, lamb, salt, 1 tbsp cumin, and 1 tbsp paprika.
2. Shape the mix into meatballs (12) with your hands.
3. Begin to stir fry your onions and garlic in a Dutch oven, in oil and butter for 7 mins then stir in the bay leaf, cumin, saffron, paprika, ginger, and pepper flakes.
4. Let the mix cook for 4 mins then stir in the tomatoes and cook them for 12 mins while breaking everything into pieces.
5. Combine in the meatballs and place a lid on the pot.
6. Cook the meat for 12 mins then crack your eggs directly into the tagine. Then layer your olives around everything.
7. Let the mix cook for 10 mins. Then top everything with the parsley.
8. Enjoy.

BUTTERNUT
Tagine

🍲 Prep Time: 15 mins

🕐 Total Time: 45 mins

Servings per Recipe: 4
Calories   123.8
Cholesterol   0.0mg
Sodium   455.3mg
Carbohydrates   23.2g
Protein   2.8g

Ingredients

2 tsps paprika
1 tsp ground cinnamon
3/4 tsp salt
1/2 tsp ground ginger
1/2 tsp crushed red pepper flakes
1/4 tsp fresh ground black pepper
1 (1 lb) beef shoulder, cubed
1 tbsp olive oil
4 shallots, quartered
4 garlic cloves, diced
1/2 C. chicken broth

1 (14 1/2 oz.) can diced tomatoes
1 lb butternut squash, cubed and skin removed
1/4 C. diced fresh cilantro

Directions

1. Get a bowl, combine: paprika, ground cinnamon, salt, ginger, pepper flakes, and black pepper.
2. Stir the spices then add in your beef and stir the meat to evenly coat everything.
3. Begin to stir fry your shallots for 7 mins, in a Dutch oven, in oil.
4. Then stir in the garlic and cook it for 2 mins then add the tomatoes and broth.
5. Get everything boiling and let the mix cook for 7 mins then add in your squash.
6. Place a lid on the pot, set the heat to low and continue to cook the mix for 17 mins.
7. Top everything with cilantro before serving.
8. Enjoy.

Cranberry and Apricot Tagine

Prep Time: 5 h
Total Time: 5 h 30 mins

Servings per Recipe: 8
Calories	380 kcal
Fat	15.2 g
Carbohydrates	38.5g
Protein	22.3 g
Cholesterol	65 mg
Sodium	571 mg

Ingredients

2 tbsps olive oil
8 skinless, boneless chicken thighs, chunked
1 eggplant, chunked
2 large onions, diced
4 large carrots, diced
1/2 C. dried cranberries
1/2 C. diced dried apricots
2 C. chicken broth
2 tbsps tomato paste
2 tbsps lemon juice

2 tbsps all-purpose flour
2 tsps garlic salt
1 1/2 tsps ground cumin
1 1/2 tsps ground ginger
1 tsp cinnamon
3/4 tsp ground black pepper
1 C. water
1 C. couscous

Directions

1. Brown your chicken all over in olive oil along with the eggplants as well.
2. Once everything is browned place it in the crock pot.
3. Add the following on top of the chicken: apricots, onions, cranberries, and carrots.
4. Get a bowl, combine: black pepper, broth, cinnamon, tomato paste, ginger, lemon juice, cumin, flour, and garlic salt.
5. Add the wet mix to the slow cooker as well.
6. Place a lid on the crock pot and cook everything for 5 hrs on high.
7. When 1 hour is left in the cooking time get your water boiling.
8. Once it is boiling add in the couscous.
9. Place a lid on the pot, and shut the heat.
10. Let the couscous stand in the water for 7 mins. Then stir it.
11. Serve the chicken on top of the couscous.
12. Enjoy.

OLIVES
and Fig Tagine
(Vegetarian)

Prep Time: 45 mins
Total Time: 2 hr 45 mins

Servings per Recipe: 8
Calories   135.8
Cholesterol   0.0mg
Sodium   317.8mg
Carbohydrates   24.3g
Protein   4.6g

Ingredients
1 red onion, diced
2 garlic cloves, diced
2 tbsps cinnamon
2 tbsps black mustard seeds
2 tbsps dried coriander
4 C. vegetable broth
2 C. cooked chickpeas
1 C. black kalamata olive, divided
1/4 C. fresh coriander, diced
8 dried figs, diced

4 C. fresh Baby Spinach

Directions
1. Set your oven to 350 degrees before doing anything else.
2. Stir fry your red onions until they are tender in olive oil, in a large pot, then add in the garlic and continue stir frying everything for 2 more mins.
3. Get a bowl, combine: coriander, cinnamon, and mustard seed.
4. Create a well in the red onion mix then pour in the cinnamon mix.
5. Let the spice toast for 1 min then stir everything together.
6. Combine in the veggie broth and chickpeas.
7. Get everything boiling with a medium level of heat then stir in the olives and place a lid on the pot.
8. Let the contents cook for 5 mins then place everything in the oven for 60 mins.
9. At the same time get a bowl, combine: figs, coriander, and spinach.
10. Once the tagine has cooked for 60 mins add in the fig mix and cook everything for 90 more mins with the lid on the pot.
11. Enjoy.

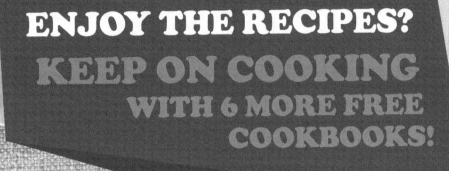

Made in the USA
Columbia, SC
27 March 2020